T0413228

AMAZING SCIENCE
WEATHER

Written by
Rebecca Phillips-Bartlett

Genius Kid

North Star
KIDS

Weather © 2024 BookLife Publishing
This edition is published by arrangement with BookLife Publishing

sales@northstareditions.com I 888-417-0195

Library of Congress Control Number:
2024952956

ISBN
978-1-952455-28-5 (library bound)
978-1-952455-84-1 (paperback)
978-1-952455-66-7 (epub)
978-1-952455-48-3 (hosted ebook)

Printed in the United States of America
Mankato, MN
092025

Written by:
Rebecca Phillips-Bartlett

Edited by:
Elise Carraway

Designed by:
Ker Ker Lee

All facts, statistics, web addresses and URLs in this book were verified as valid and accurate at time of writing. No responsibility for any changes to external websites or references can be accepted by either the author or publisher.

Photo Credits – Images courtesy of Shutterstock.com, unless otherwise stated.

Cover – Brum, Nataliia K, Jessica2, Pornsawan Baipakdee, Andy Chairil, J.J. Gouin, New Africa, Irina Gutyryak, Jade ThaiCatwalk, plampy, Tatiana Popova, Tomas Ragina, yingko, merrymuuu, Alexey Kljatov. 2–3 – na-um, Pixel-Shot. 4–5 – Steve Heap, Evgenyrychko, Antero Aaltonen, Nazarii_ Neshcherenskyi, Kokhan O. 6–7 – Tomas Ragina, MJfotografie.cz, 19 STUDIO, Potapov Alexander. 8–9 – vovan, Shuttercountproduction, Studio Romantic, Fotovika, New Africa. 10–11 – Allexxandar, Tomas Nevesely, Yashi S007, Alexandra Bobir. 12–13 – Wichai Prasomsri1, Lucas Rizzi, New Africa. 14–15 – Melidis Alexandros, OSORIOartist, Grey Zone. 16–17 – Michele Ursi, Pande Putu Hadi Wiguna. 18–19 – domnitsky, trancedrumer, Piyaset, Rasulov, Ljupco Smokovski. 20–21 – Cast Of Thousands, Le Dang Nhut Minh, Jade ThaiCatwalk, Roxana Bashyrova, Sarah Quintans. 22–23 – AYO Production, AYO Production, nednapa, Tatiana Popova, IDEA ROUTE, Tomas Ragina, LilKar.

CONTENTS

Words that look like <u>this</u> can be found in the glossary on page 24.

THE WEATHER

Look out the window. What can you see?

Is the sun shining, or is it covered by clouds? Can you see any raindrops falling from the sky? Are the trees swaying in the wind?

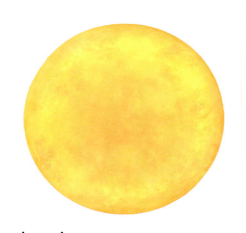

Sunny, cloudy, rainy, and windy are all types of weather.

4

Weather is what is happening in the sky and air outside. Weather can change quickly. It can also stay the same for days.

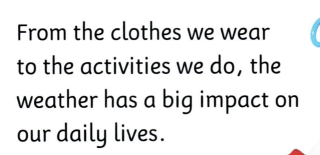

From the clothes we wear to the activities we do, the weather has a big impact on our daily lives.

KEY WORDS

There are some key words that every genius kid should learn.

TEMPERATURE
Temperature is how hot or cold something is.

PRECIPITATION
Precipitation is any water or frozen water that falls from the sky to Earth. It includes rain, snow, and hail.

CLIMATE

Climate is the usual weather in an area over many years. It includes the usual temperature and amount of precipitation.

SEASONS

Seasons are ways of splitting the year up based on the weather. Spring, summer, fall, and winter are seasons. Some places have a wet season and a dry season.

SUNSHINE

The sun gives off heat and light called sunshine. Sunshine is what makes life on Earth possible.

Our bodies use sunshine to make vitamin D. Vitamin D helps our bones grow strong.

Plants use sunshine to make their food.

Humans need sunshine. However, too much sun can be harmful.

People should not stay in the sunshine too long. They should make sure to wear sunscreen to protect their skin.

DID YOU KNOW?
We can use sunshine to make electricity. Electricity made using sunshine is called solar power.

RAIN

Rain is part of the water cycle. The water cycle is the journey water takes as it moves around Earth.

COLLECTION
Rainwater flows along the ground. It collects in rivers, lakes, and other bodies of water.

PRECIPITATION
Raindrops in clouds grow until they are too heavy to stay in the sky. Then they fall as precipitation.

EVAPORATION
When water gets warm, it turns into a <u>gas</u> called water vapor. Water vapor rises.

CONDENSATION
High in the sky, water vapor cools down and turns back into water. These tiny drops of water make clouds.

WIND

Wind is the movement of air.

Sunshine heats the air. Some air gets warmer than other air. Warmer air is lighter than cooler air. It rises in the sky. Cooler air rushes to fill the gap the warm air leaves. This rush of cool air is the wind.

Warm air rises.

Cool air fills the gap.

Wind can cause many changes in the weather. Wind can blow rain clouds across the sky to new areas.

Gentle winds are safe. However, strong winds can blow things over and cause damage.

WILD WEATHER

THUNDER AND LIGHTNING

In clouds, pieces of ice bump into one another. This causes <u>charges</u> to build up in different parts of the cloud. If the charges grow strong enough, a flash and a bang happen. The flash is called lightning. The bang is thunder.

HURRICANES

Hurricanes start as strong winds over warm oceans. The wind swirls around, creating a <u>tropical storm</u>.

TORNADOES

Tornadoes are tubes of strong, spinning wind that form over land. They stretch from storm clouds down to the ground.

15

A TIMELINE OF WEATHER FORECASTING

Weather forecasting is when scientists use <u>evidence</u> to figure out what the weather will be.

340 BCE
Aristotle wrote books full of his ideas about rain, clouds, and storms.

1861
FitzRoy released the first public weather forecast.

1854
A ship's captain, called Robert FitzRoy, started to work out how to use science for weather forecasting. He wanted to make life at sea safer.

1920s
The radiosonde was <u>invented</u>. A radiosonde is a box full of equipment which is sent into the sky to collect information. Radiosondes are still used today.

1960
NASA sent the first weather <u>satellite</u> into space.

CLIMATE CHANGE

Our climate has always been changing. However, in the last 150 years, Earth has started getting hotter much more quickly. People have started burning more <u>fossil fuels</u> to power factories and vehicles. Burning fossil fuels releases harmful gases that trap heat and warm Earth up.

This long-term change to Earth's climate is called climate change.

Climate change makes the weather more extreme and harder to forecast.

Long-term weather changes make it harder for many animals and plants to live.

BELIEVE IT OR NOT!

The coldest recorded temperature on Earth was –128 degrees Fahrenheit.

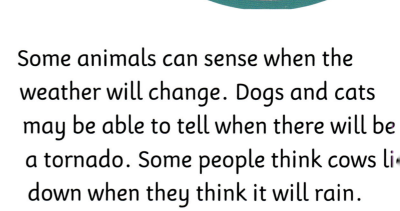

Some animals can sense when the weather will change. Dogs and cats may be able to tell when there will be a tornado. Some people think cows li down when they think it will rain.

Fog is clouds that are very close to the ground.

You can figure out how far away a storm is by counting the seconds between seeing the lightning and hearing the thunder. Count the seconds. Your answer is how many miles away the storm is.

ARE YOU A GENIUS KID?

You should now be full of facts to impress your friends. But are you really a genius kid? There is only one way to find out! Let's put your knowledge to the test.

Check back through the book if you are not sure.

1. What is another word for rain or snow?

2. Why did Robert FitzRoy start working on the science of weather forecasting?

3. What is climate change?

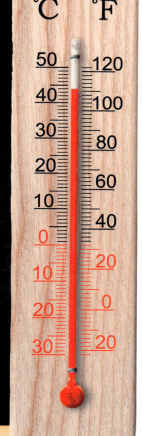

GLOSSARY

charges the amounts of electricity in something, often described as being either positive or negative

evidence facts that can be used to prove something

fossil fuels fuels, such as coal, oil, and gas, that formed millions of years ago from the remains of animals and plants

gas a thing that is like air, which spreads out to fill any space available

invented when something new is made for the first time

satellite a machine that travels around a planet or moon, often taking photos and collecting information

tropical storm a storm with spinning winds that forms over the ocean and is not as strong as a hurricane but can grow to become one

INDEX